≈ Primary Sources of American Treaties™ ≈

The Transcontinental Treaty, 1819

A Primary Source Examination of the Treaty Between the United States and Spain Over the American West

Meg Greene

rosen central
Primary Source™
The Rosen Publishing Group, Inc., New York

For my father

Published in 2006 by The Rosen Publishing Group, Inc.
29 East 21st Street, New York, NY 10010

First Edition

Library of Congress Cataloging-in-Publication Data

Greene, Meg.
The Transcontinental Treaty, 1819: a primary source examination of the treaty between the United States and Spain over the American West / Meg Greene.
 p. cm.—(Primary sources of American treaties)
Includes bibliographical references and index.
ISBN 1-4042-0439-3 (lib. bdg.)
1. United States—Foreign relations—Spain—Juvenile literature. 2. Spain—Foreign relations—United States—Juvenile literature. 3. Spain. Treaties, etc. United States, 1819 Feb. 22—Juvenile literature. 4. United States—Foreign relations—1817–1825—Juvenile literature. 5. United States—Foreign relations—1809–1817—Juvenile literature. I. Title. II. Series.
E183.8.S7G68 2005
327.73046'09'034—dc22

2004027816

Manufactured in the United States of America

On the cover: An etching and engraving (circa 1770s) illustrating a view of Pensacola, in West Florida, drawn by George Gauld.

Contents

Introduction

uring 1818 and 1819, two men carried on a series of difficult negotiations. At stake was the gaining of an important piece of territory for a new nation and the struggle of an old power to hang on to what was left of its once magnificent empire. The result of these negotiations was the Transcontinental Treaty of 1819, which is also known as the Adams-Onís Treaty. The treaty was named for the American secretary of state John Quincy Adams and the Spanish minister to the United States Don Luis de Onís y Gonzales, the two men who negotiated the treaty terms.

The Transcontinental Treaty, signed on George Washington's birthday, February 22, 1819, ended more than a quarter century of diplomatic rivalry between the United States and Spain. For the United States, the agreement helped to define the western boundary of the country and to further the American quest to become an owner of a great empire that extended from coast to coast. For the Spanish, the treaty was principally a means of saving what remained of the Spanish Empire in North America, specifically Texas and the Southwest. The Spanish also hoped that the treaty would prevent the United States government from recognizing the independence of the rebellious Spanish colonies in South America.

The negotiations were often frustratingly slow and uncertain. Ultimately, however, the treaty gave both the Americans and the Spanish some amount of success. As a result of the treaty, the United States acquired Florida. The Spanish, for the time being, kept Texas. For both countries, the treaty offered an opportunity to settle claims that had resulted from earlier wars. Perhaps most important to the United States government was the recognition of a boundary between Spanish and American territory that extended from the Gulf of Mexico to the Pacific Ocean.

The Americans also believed that the Transcontinental Treaty promised a greater sense of safety to a nation that was open to attack from European power. For years, the United States government had eyed Spanish Florida with growing anxiety. The Americans had long feared the presence of foreign enemies so close to American borders. The U.S. government knew that the Spanish grip on North America was growing weaker. What the Americans feared most was the possibility of another more powerful enemy crossing from Florida to invade the United States. Acquiring Florida decreased security concerns for the U.S. government and particularly for the states up and down the Atlantic seaboard.

Yet, in some ways, the question of the western boundary was of even greater importance. Both Spain and the United States wished for easy access to the Pacific. The Spanish

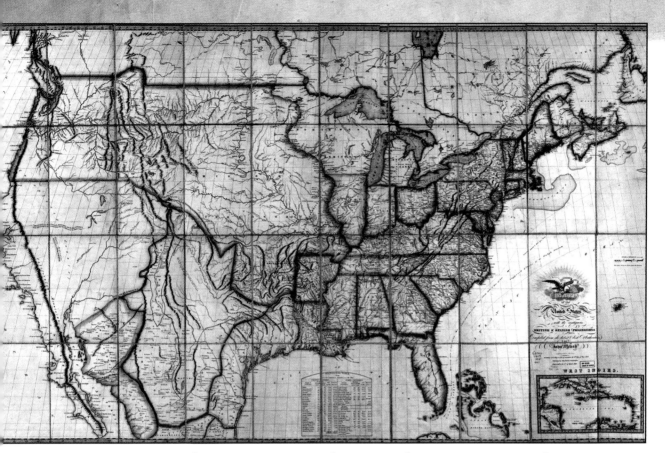

This map of the United States of America, from 1816, was the first that showed the entire country. It outlines the parts of the country that were under the control of the British and the Spanish. An earlier edition of this same map was used during the negotiations of the Transcontinental Treaty.

---

assumed that the entire Pacific coast belonged to them. However, in making such a claim, they did not take into account the English and Russian presence in the Pacific Northwest. Meanwhile, the Americans wanted to establish their presence in the West. Specifically, they wanted to expand the territory of the United States all the way to the Pacific Ocean. Many Americans, including John Quincy Adams, believed in America's "manifest destiny," or the inescapable fate of the United States to become an enormous continental empire. The Transcontinental Treaty, Adams believed, was a sure means of continuing the process of ports of Spain or of her Colonies, shall be admitted for the term of twelve years to the ports of Pensacola and St. Augustine in the Floridas, without paying other or higher duties on their cargoes or of tonnage than will be paid by the vessels of the United States — During the said term no other Nation shall enjoy the same privileges within the ceded territories. — The twelve years shall commence three months after the exchange of the Ratifications of this Treaty.

Art. 16.

The present Treaty shall be ratified in due form by the contracting parties, and the Ratifications shall be exchanged in six months from this time, or sooner if possible.

In witness whereof, we the Underwritten Plenipotentiaries of the United States of America and of His Catholic Majesty, have signed, by virtue of our powers, the present Treaty of Amity, Settlement and Limits, and have thereunto affixed our Seals respectively.

Done at Washington this twenty second day of February one thousand eight hundred and nineteen.

John Quincy Adams.

Luis de Onis

This is a copy of the Transcontinental Treaty. In signing and ratifying the treaty, John Quincy Adams and Don Luis de Onís y Gonzales ultimately set the boundaries for an area of land (from the western banks of the Sabine, Red, and Arkansas rivers to the Continental Divide) that was very beneficial for the United States. See page 54 for an excerpt from the treaty.

American expansion. What makes the settlement of the western boundary so extraordinary is that, at best, both the Spanish and the Americans had only slight knowledge of the territory they were trying to define. In other words, Adams and Onís were bargaining over land that they had never seen and about which they knew very little.

The signing of the Transcontinental Treaty indicated the growing influence of the United States as a world power. By this time, the more powerful European governments, such as those of France and England, had no desire to help Spain. They wanted the Spanish Empire and the Spanish kingdom to be further weakened. This meant that Spain would no longer be a threat to other countries. And for many European nations, having more friendly relations with the United States was simply more important than helping Spain. For the Americans, the treaty emphasized the growing sense that the future of the United States lay in westward expansion, which, in time, would make the United States the most powerful nation on Earth.

s of Spain or of her Colonies, sha
rs to the ports of Pensacola and
out paying other or higher duties

1

The Spanish and the New World

In their search to find a shorter, cheaper route to the Far East, the Spanish accidentally discovered two continents that no one in Europe knew about. Even the man who came upon these lands, explorer Christopher Columbus, insisted that he had found a more direct route to India, the Spice Islands, and Cathay (China). However, Columbus was wrong. Nonetheless, Spain benefited from his error and soon claimed much of North and South America. This was the beginning of one of the greatest and most powerful empires in the world.

⌐ Imperial Spain ⌐

Columbus had tried to persuade various European kingdoms to accept his idea that there was a shorter trade route to the Far East. Unfortunately, as Columbus explained his plans, the only response was disbelief and rejection. But when Columbus approached the queen and king of Spain, Isabella of Castile and Ferdinand of Aragon, he received a very different response. Queen Isabella already knew of the great riches and money that the neighboring Portuguese

This engraving depicts explorer Christopher Columbus bidding farewell to King Ferdinand II of Spain and his wife, Queen Isabella I. Columbus, who was born in 1451 in Genoa, Italy, is about to set off on the voyage during which he would discover the New World. In the background, sailors can be seen heading out to board Columbus's three ships.

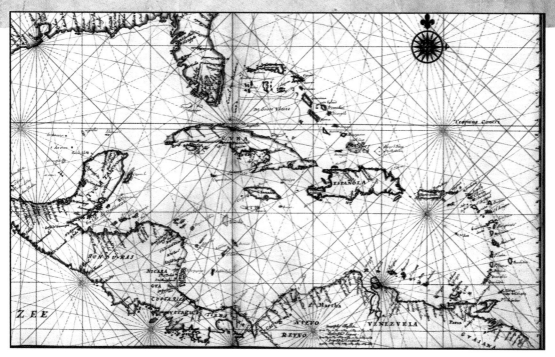

This map shows the lands that Columbus discovered. The islands of Cuba (left) and Puerto Rico (right) are outlined in yellow; Espanola (or Hispaniola), which is present-day Haiti and the Dominican Republic, is outlined in red. The map also depicts the coasts of North and South America including the Yucatán peninsula in Mexico and Guiana in South America.

had made from their explorations in Africa, India, and the Far East. She was hoping for even greater success with Columbus's plan. The Spanish also realized that with the 1544 proclamation by Pope Nicholas V that granted Portugal complete control of Africa and areas of Asia, the Spanish had to strike out in another direction if they wished to succeed. Columbus's proposal offered an opportunity to do so.

With financial support from the Spanish crown, Columbus set sail in August 1492 with three ships, the *Niña*, the *Pinta*, and the *Santa Maria*. He had a fair wind, and after just thirty-three days of uneventful sailing, his lookout sighted land in what is now the Bahamas. Columbus first came ashore in the New World on an island that he christened

THE GOLDEN AGE

Guided by the leadership of Ferdinand of Aragon and Isabella of Castile, Spain became an international power. As a result of their efforts and accomplishments, their grandson, Charles I, not only inherited a New World empire but also a European one as well. This included the Kingdom of Spain, the Netherlands, Austria, Sardinia, Sicily, the Kingdom of Naples, parts of Germany, and Franche-Comté, an area now located in the east of France.

In 1519, Charles was elected Holy Roman Emperor and became Charles V, the most powerful monarch in Europe. However, the continual warfare in places such as Italy and the Germanys drained Spain of its resources. Charles's son, Philip II, struggled to preserve the empire he had inherited.

Nonetheless, the English defeat of the Spanish Armada in 1588 marked the beginning of the end of the Spanish power. By 1660, the "golden age" of Spain was over.

Italian painter Titian's portrait of Charles V dates from 1533. Charles appointed Titian court painter because the emperor was so pleased with this painting. Titian was one of the most important and influential painters during the period of art known as the High Renaissance.

San Salvador, "Our Savior." He also explored the coastline of Cuba and the northern shores of an island that he called Hispaniola, "Little Spain," which is modern-day Haiti and the Dominican Republic.

It was not long before the Spanish became the dominant power in the New World, gaining control of its land and its wealth. By 1550, the Spanish Empire stretched over the whole of Central and South America (except Brazil) and included a large portion of North America. The Spanish owed their control of the Americas to no more than a few thousand adventurers and soldiers. In overrunning the Western Hemisphere, the conquistadores became the masters of hundreds of thousands of native peoples and crushed the powerful military empires of the Aztecs in Mexico and the Incas in Peru and northern Chile.

⟿ Spanish Florida ⟿

In 1513, although Juan Ponce de León sailed into the Bahía de Espíritu Santo (the Bay of the Holy Spirit, known today as Tampa Bay), he did not establish a permanent Spanish settlement in North America. Fifteen years later, in 1528, following the Spanish conquests of Mexico and Peru, Pánfilo de Narváez also failed to secure the Spanish hold on *La Florida*. Driven off by a series of fierce Indian attacks, Narváez and his group of explorers survived only to drown in a hurricane off the gulf coast of Texas while making their escape. Between 1539 and 1543, Hernando de Soto explored the interior of Florida as well as much of the region that became the southeastern United States.

The de Soto expedition was the most extensive the Spanish had yet undertaken in North America. It was also among the most disastrous.

The harsh heat, unending hunger, worsening fatigue, rough terrain, numerous insects, and angry Indians soon took their toll on the Spanish. During the winter of 1539 and 1540, de Soto and his men made camp at the Indian town of Anhaica (present-day Tallahassee). Once spring arrived, they moved north into Georgia and Carolina. Turning westward and possibly traveling as far as Louisiana, de Soto sought to return to Florida. He hoped that by reaching the Bay of Ochuse (modern Pensacola) by the end of October, he and his men could meet up with the ships of Captain Francisco Maldonado and take on needed supplies. But on October 18, 1540, Chief Tuzcaluza, who was known as Black Warrior, attacked the Spanish near Mauvilla, located in what is today central Alabama. The Spanish claimed victory but suffered terrible losses.

After the Battle of Mauvilla, de Soto, wishing to avoid disgrace, refused to proceed to Ochuse and instead led his battered and demoralized forces westward, toward the Mississippi River, becoming the first European ever to lay eyes on the mighty river. During 1542, de Soto explored Arkansas and Texas while desperately searching for deposits of gold or silver. Then he returned to the Mississippi, where he died on May 21, 1543. Under the leadership of Luis de Moscoso, about half of the original 700 conquistadores who had accompanied de Soto eventually made their way back to Spain.

Like those of Ponce de León and Narváez, de Soto's expedition to Florida ended in failure. He had not found any empires to conquer nor any wealth to exploit. As well, he failed to establish a Spanish settlement in the region. Not until the founding of St. Augustine in 1565 did the Spanish have a colony in Florida. Although the Spanish were disappointed in their progress, the Spanish settlement at St. Augustine came before the English settlement at Jamestown, Virginia, by more than forty years. Nevertheless, for more than half a century, the Spanish had struggled to control southeastern North America. And after 1565, they still had little to show for their efforts in finding treasure and territory.

⸺ A Possession Passed Back and Forth ⸺

In part because of the fragile Spanish hold on Florida, the colony became the center of conflict between the three powers vying for control of North America. In 1719, the French captured and briefly held the Spanish settlement at Pensacola. After the Spanish regained Pensacola, the threat of French conquest decreased for the time being.

The Spanish then had to contend with English buccaneers who robbed other countries' ships and attacked foreign territories, often without permission from their respective nation's rulers. One of Spain's biggest threats in the New World came from noted buccaneers such as Englishman Sir Francis Drake. Drake continually plagued the Spanish, robbing their ships of cargo and treasure. In 1586, Drake became even bolder, attacking St. Augustine. The English, determined to get their hands on Florida, attacked the territory in 1702

This engraving, illustrating an attack on Fort George, took place during the siege of Pensacola (1781). Spanish troops (shown in the foreground) profited from the attack and forced the surrender of the British camp. The battle, which commenced on March 9, ended on June 20 when the British were forced to leave.

and again in 1704. The colonial governor of Georgia, a British colony, ordered another invasion of Spanish Florida in 1740. With each new attack, however, the Spanish managed to defeat the English.

In 1763, the English at last gained control of Florida in exchange for Havana, Cuba. The British had captured Cuba from Spain during the Seven Years' War (1756–1763). The British had ambitious plans for Florida. First, they split it into two parts: East Florida, with its capital at St. Augustine, and West Florida, with its seat at Pensacola. The British government attempted to attract settlers, but ultimately it failed to entice that many. As a result, the British influence in Florida lasted for only about twenty years. With the outbreak of the American Revolution in 1775, the Spanish saw an opportunity to regain their former possession. Entering the war on the side of the Americans in 1779, the Spanish received Florida as a token of American gratitude. In 1783, the Spanish flag once again flew over Florida. By the second decade of the nineteenth century, the Spanish had been a presence in Florida for more than 300 years. However, if the Americans got their way, that was about to change.

of Spain or of her colonies, sha
s to the ports of Pensacola and
out paying other higher duties

2

The Florida Question

James Monroe was the fourth member of the "Virginia dynasty" (George Washington, Thomas Jefferson, James Madison, and James Monroe), four U.S. presidents who all came from Virginia. He was sixty-one years old when he became the fifth president of the United States in 1817. Though less respected and distinguished than his predecessors, Monroe provided his countrymen with a reassuring sense of order following the War of 1812, which ended two years before he took office.

President Monroe's optimism helped Americans to become more hopeful and gave rise to a period that became known as the era of good feelings. Yet, despite his positive outlook, Monroe was in fact bothered by both domestic and foreign problems. Among the most important was the nagging question of Florida.

⇒ A Sought-After Prize ⇒

The problem of the Spanish possession of Florida had troubled the Americans for almost three decades. With the Treaty of Paris in 1783, the boundaries of the independent

This portrait of James Monroe is a copy of a famous portrait by Thomas Sully. Monroe, known as the "era of good feelings president," studied law before being elected to the Continental Congress. After he was elected president, Monroe went on a cross-country tour and was thus seen by more Americans than any president prior to him.

United States extended south to the Florida line and west to the Mississippi River. Once again, the Spanish ruled Florida. Unfortunately, Spain had loosened its requirements for settlers there. This move cost Spain dearly as hundreds of Americans came to Florida. For the United States government, American settlement in Florida was the opening wedge that was needed to split Florida from the Spanish Empire.

Throughout the early nineteenth century, American leaders feared that whoever owned Florida "held a pistol at the heart of the Republic," as the popular saying went. European powers, jealous of America's independence and still in hot pursuit of territories in the New World, caused many Americans great anxiety. The United States government was fearful that its enemies could use Florida to begin an invasion of the United States. Soon, the U.S. government found the continued "foreign" presence on "American" soil to be unbearable. The one sure way to guarantee American security was for the United States to obtain control of Florida. The Americans wished to gain Florida without a war. Instead, in the case of Florida, the U.S. government preferred to take

THE LOUISIANA PURCHASE

In 1803, the United States made perhaps the greatest land deal in American history. For the price of $15,000,000, or less than three cents an acre, President Thomas Jefferson bought 828,000 square miles (2,145,000 kilometers). He acquired the territory from France, which had obtained it from Spain. The exact boundaries of the purchase remained uncertain. However, Jefferson believed that it stretched from the Mississippi River westward to the Rocky Mountains and from the Gulf of Mexico north to Canada. Jefferson and his secretary of state, James Madison, also claimed that the Louisiana Territory included West Florida,

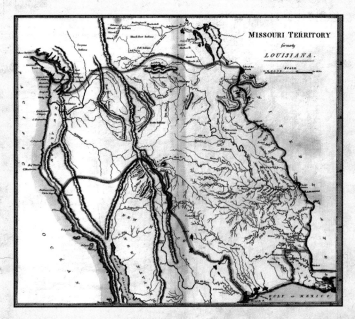

This map from 1814 outlines the land that helped the fledgling United States expand westward as a result of the terms of the Louisiana Purchase. Napoléon, the future emperor of France, was in need of money to support his armies in Europe. Thus, he decided to sell this large tract of land to the United States.

between the Mississippi and Perdido rivers. As a result of the purchase, the port of New Orleans and the Mississippi River were secured for American merchants and farmers. This meant that the country could expand westward to the Pacific Ocean.

advantage of the growing Spanish weakness in the North American territory, forcing Spain to give up Florida without a fight. One way or another, the Americans hoped that the Spanish would be willing to cede Florida. It was believed that without Florida, the United States government was at stake.

Even without pressure from the Americans, the Spanish hold on Florida was weakening as Spanish power in general continued to slip. Ironically, the American Revolution (in which the Spanish fought on the side of the Americans) had planted the seeds of revolutionary independence movements in Mexico and South America. In danger of losing their American empire, the Spanish found themselves in an uncomfortable position. Like the British in 1775, they were struggling vainly to hold on to their territory in America.

⸺ A Worsening Situation ⸺

In reality, the United States had been taking over Florida little by little for years. In 1795, Spain finally accepted the American demand to recognize the 31st parallel as the northern boundary of Florida. The Americans had also tried (without success) to purchase Florida from Spain, first in 1803 and again in 1805. By the mid-1810s, the Americans believed that they had a good case to persuade the Spanish to surrender their hold on Florida. Spain had not lived up to its obligations under the Pinckney Treaty of 1795. This treaty required the Spanish to restrain attacks by the Indians living in Florida. Distracted by the unrest in Mexico and South America, the Spanish did little—and, in truth, there was little that they could do to protect American settlers from Indian raids. The United States government held the Spanish directly responsible for the actions of the Indians. It made it clear that if Spain did nothing to stop the violence, the United States would be forced to interfere.

A precedent already existed for such action. In January 1811, army deserters, fugitive slaves, and Spanish, English, and American planters rebelled against Spanish authority. They established the Republic of West Florida. Congress then authorized President Madison to seize the area west of the Perdido River. By 1813, the United States had taken most of West Florida from Spain. Shortly thereafter, the American government also encouraged rebellion in East Florida. Despite the failure of that rebellion, the Spanish hold on East Florida was so shaky that it was only a matter of time before it, too, passed to the control of the United States government.

⇌ Postponing the Final Outcome ⇌

As a result of such incidents and disputes, American relations with Spain continued to get worse. In the middle of these tensions, Don Luis de Onís y Gonzales arrived in Washington in 1815 to serve as Spanish minister to the United States. As a representative of the Spanish crown and protector of the

Spanish Empire in America, Onís was supposed to guard Texas, New Mexico, and Florida, the Spanish territories that bordered the United States. Onís also tried to convince the Americans to stay out of Spanish affairs in Mexico and South America. If the Americans refused to aid or recognize the revolutionaries, Onís made it clear that Spain might be willing to talk about Florida. But under no circumstances did Onís intend to make life easy for the Americans. Exercising a stubborn will by constantly delaying talks and making vague promises, Onís enjoyed annoying American officials for the next four years.

⟨ A Worthy Opponent ⟩

When Onís began talks with Secretary of State (and soon to be President) James Monroe in 1817, he quickly sensed how badly the Americans wanted Florida. An experienced diplomat, Onís realized that he had an important bargaining chip. In discussing the boundaries of the Louisiana Purchase of 1803, both Onís and Monroe were aware that the boundaries were unclear. Onís told Monroe that the Spanish government regarded the Louisiana Purchase as a giant fraud. Onís then reassured Monroe that Spain would give up its claim to Florida. In return, the United States would agree to set the western boundary of the Louisiana Purchase at the Mississippi River, thereby protecting the Spanish hold on territory from Texas westward.

After Monroe became president in 1816, Onís's negotiating partner was John Quincy Adams. Monroe had named Adams as secretary of state. The son of John Adams, an

John Quincy Adams is pictured here after signing the Treaty of Ghent. Article I of the treaty stated, "There shall be a firm and universal peace between His Britannic Majesty and the United States, and between their respective Countries, Territories, Cities, Towns, and People of every degree without exception of places or persons."

important leader in the American struggle for independence and later the second president of the United States, John Quincy Adams had already enjoyed an outstanding diplomatic career. He had served as American minister to the Netherlands, Prussia, and Russia. As well, he was one of five American officials to negotiate the Treaty of Ghent. This treaty had brought an end to the War of 1812. Adams, who was a senator from Massachusetts, was also the minister to Great Britain when Monroe summoned him to become secretary of state.

By the time Adams took office, Onís had revised his position. The Americans wanted to set the boundary of the Louisiana Purchase at the Mississippi River. As Onís explained to Monroe, the Spanish government now wished for the boundary to be drawn farther east, between the Mermentau and Calcasieu rivers, located in central Louisiana. Adams then offered the Spanish a western boundary along the Colorado River in Texas. Of course, both the Americans and the Spanish wanted to get as much as they could while giving away as little as possible. For the time being, negotiations

MEMOIR
UPON THE
NEGOTIATIONS BETWEEN SPAIN
AND
THE UNITED STATES OF AMERICA,
WHICH
LED TO THE TREATY OF 1819.
WITH
A STATISTICAL NOTICE OF THAT COUNTRY.
ACCOMPANIED WITH AN APPENDIX,
CONTAINING IMPORTANT DOCUMENTS FOR THE BETTER
ILLUSTRATION OF THE SUBJECT.
BY D. LUIS DE ONIS,
Late Minister Plenipotentiary near that Republick, and present Embassador
from H. M. at the Court of Naples.

MADRID, 1820.
From the Press of D. M. De Burgos.

Translated from the Spanish, with Notes,
BY TOBIAS WATKINS.

This is the title page of Memoir Upon the Negotiations Between Spain and the United States of America, Which Led to the Treaty of 1819, *written by Don Luis de Onís in 1820. This leather-bound book with gilt (gold) lettering was translated from Spanish into English. See page 55 for an excerpt from the book.*

came to a deadlock as Onís withdrew to consider Adams's proposal and to communicate with his government. It took the actions of an American general to get both men talking again.

⌐ Pushing Harder ⌐

Monroe then made the decision to invade Florida. A successful invasion would punish the Seminole Indians who had been raiding American frontier outposts in Florida. The invasion would also reinforce Adams's diplomatic efforts to negotiate the transfer of Florida from Spain to the United States. With Monroe's approval, Secretary of War John C. Calhoun then ordered General Andrew Jackson to invade Florida. Calhoun's orders were backed up by a secret letter to Monroe from Jackson. In the letter, Monroe instructed, "The movement against the Seminoles . . . will bring you on a theatre [place] where you may possibly have other services to perform . . . Great interests are at issue."

Jackson thought Monroe's instructions gave him permission to invade Florida. Not only would the invasion punish the Seminoles, but it would also lead to a defeat of the Spanish. If the Americans succeeded in taking Florida, it would give them an advantage in the treaty talks with the Spanish. For this mission, Jackson didn't need to have much tactical skill. Instead, he needed a great amount of confidence, stubbornness, and fierce determination, traits that he clearly had.

⇁The Invasion of Florida ⇁

Jackson and his troops plunged into Florida early in March 1818. On April 6, American forces seized the Spanish fort of St. Marks. From there, Jackson pushed his men further into the gloomy forests and uncharted swamps of Florida. At sunset on April 18, Jackson's forces attacked the Seminole village of Chief Boleck, or "Bowlegs" as the Americans called him. However, they found it to be nearly deserted. After an unsuccessful search for the Indians, Jackson and his men began the journey back to St. Marks on April 21. Accompanying Jackson as a prisoner was Lieutenant Robert C. Ambrister, formerly an officer in the British Royal Colonial Marines. (He had been suspended from active duty for dueling with a fellow officer.) Ambrister was captured along with a white servant and two blacks when he accidentally stumbled into Jackson's picket lines (a detachment of one or more troops who warn of an enemy's approach).

A search of Lieutenant Ambrister and his attendants uncovered documents suggesting that another man, Scottish merchant and British subject Alexander Arbuthnot, had

The swampland of Florida was not the most welcoming environment for General Jackson and his men. Seen above is a watercolor painting of the kind of wild and unchartered territory the American troops would have had to contend with. Tropical diseases such as yellow fever were rampant, wild animals were a constant threat, and the sweltering heat added to the difficulties of the journey.

warned Chief Boleck and his people of the American plans to attack their village. Jackson, who already had Arbuthnot in custody at St. Marks, believed that both Ambrister and Arbuthnot were foreign agents. He thought they had turned the Seminoles against the Americans, which ultimately led to their own ruin. A special military court that convened at St. Marks on April 26 condemned both Ambrister and Arbuthnot to death on charges of aiding the enemies of the United States. With Jackson's approval, the sentences were carried out on April 29; Ambrister went before a firing squad and Arbuthnot was hanged. Jackson believed he had made the right choice in executing Ambrister and Arbuthnot. He did not seem concerned that news of his actions would annoy the British and lead to calls for revenge against the United States. Instead of such worries, he was planning his next move. This would be a daring and dangerous adventure against the Spanish.

On May 24, a little less than a month after the executions of Ambrister and Arbuthnot, American troops attacked and occupied the Spanish fort at St. Michael. The fort overlooked Pensacola, the capital of Spanish Florida. Five days later, on May 29, Jackson captured Pensacola. He met little resistance from Spanish forces, who were under the command of colonial governor Don Jose Masot. At home, reports of Jackson's actions and behavior enhanced the public popularity he already enjoyed as a result of his victory over the British at the Battle of New Orleans in January 1815. However, politically, Jackson's successful campaign in Florida complicated Adams's negotiations with the Spanish. Nonetheless, Adams stood and defended Jackson's actions. He argued that in attacking the Indians, executing two British subjects, and capturing St. Marks and Pensacola, Jackson had carried out his orders.

Adams not only refused to apologize to the British or the Spanish for Jackson's behavior, but he even went so far as to tell Spanish officials that they, and not the Americans, were responsible for all that had taken place in Florida. As Adams noted, it was the Spanish who had failed to keep the peace and preserve order. They had no one but themselves to blame for the current state of affairs. Adams insisted that Spain must either govern Florida responsibly or turn the territory over to the United States. He declared in a letter that Spanish Florida had become "a derelict [neglected place], open to the occupying of every enemy, civilized or savage, of the United States, and serving no other earthly purpose than as a post of annoyance to them."

⚊ Monroe's Ultimatum ⚊

After some hesitation, Monroe eventually agreed with Adams. As a result, Madison issued an ultimatum to the Spanish government. The Spanish would have to send a military unit to Florida to maintain sufficient order. Monroe knew the Spanish would have difficulty doing this. The other option was to cede Florida to the United States, which could govern it properly. Though the Spanish government was in no condition to accept this challenge, it was also in no position to resist it. Onís protested, demanding financial compensation from the United States for American outrages against Spanish honor, property, and life. In the end, he and his government had little choice but to give in to American demands. Spain would eventually yield to the Americans another piece of the once magnificent empire it had held in the New World since the sixteenth century.

3

Coming to an Agreement

lthough their empire in North and South America was crumbling, the Spanish continued to resist American efforts to acquire Florida. On instructions from the Spanish foreign minister José Garcia de Leon y Pizarro, Onís announced that his government would not sign a treaty with the United States until Florida was restored to Spanish authority. Nonetheless, he continued to meet with Adams. Onís also objected to what the Spanish considered to be the outrageous behavior of General Jackson. However, they could do nothing except make further boundary concessions in the west if necessary.

⇒ The Talks Continue ⇒

Adams and Onís were engaged in a game of diplomatic cat-and-mouse, each taking care not to reveal too much to the other. Both men wished to avoid a war, but neither wanted to give their opponent any advantage. For example, in discussions with Onís on July 11, 1818, Adams again insisted that the boundary between the United States and Spanish territory be drawn at the Colorado River in central

Texas. At the same time, Adams informed Onís that the United States government was willing to set the northern boundary of Spanish territory at latitude 45°20'. This is where Adams believed the Missouri River originated. (However, he was incorrect. The source of the Missouri is actually farther north, in the present state of Montana.) Five days later, on July 16, Adams told the French minister to the United States, Jean-Guillaume Hyde de Neuville, that he was prepared to move the boundary further east to the Trinity River. This would enlarge Spanish holdings in the West. But Adams also explained to Baron de Neuville that he would then adjust the northern boundary of Spanish territory to latitude 41°30', which Adams (mistakenly) believed was the source of the Rio Bravo del Norte (now the Rio Grande). To both Onís and de Neuville, Adams proposed drawing the boundary line all the way to the Pacific Ocean. Onís immediately rejected this offer. Despite a British and Russian presence in the Pacific Northwest, the Spanish claimed the entire Pacific coast as far north as the 56th parallel, which crosses present-day British Columbia.

Meanwhile, Spanish foreign minister Pizarro had communicated to Onís a willingness to give up Florida. The Spanish had come to regard the territory as indefensible, and they thought perhaps the United States would be willing to move the western boundary of Spanish territory from the Calcasieu and Mermentau rivers in central Louisiana to just west of the Sabine River in Texas. If Adams had not revealed to Onís the willingness of the Americans to set the boundary east of the Trinity River, Onís in turn would not have told Adams that

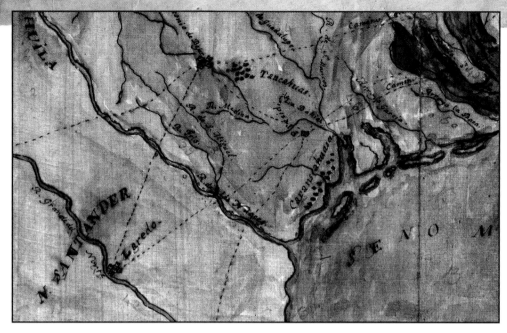

This map dating from 1822 was created by Stephen Austin soon after American settlers had arrived in Texas. Austin, the founder of Texas, created a colony here after receiving clearance from the Spanish government to do so. This map shows the territory of the Mexican state of Texas as well as the Rio del Norte river when it was a part of Mexican territory.

the Spanish would agree to setting it west of the Sabine. However, Adams did tell Onís that if the Spanish gave up Florida, President Monroe would not press for the immediate settlement of the western boundary.

Although Adams thought he was offering a concession to Spain in leaving the western boundary undecided, Adams's proposal was unacceptable to Onís. Fearing further American intrusion on Spanish territory in the West, Onís felt that his government could not allow the question of the western boundary to linger. At a minimum, he needed to protect Texas from a possible American invasion. However, he also hoped to keep the whole of the southwest from falling under American control. In exchange for determining the western boundary of Spanish territory in North America, Onís offered Florida.

According to George Langefield's book, *The Era of Good Feelings* (1952), during their meeting, Onís told Adams that the western boundary was "the sole object of the sacrifices which His Majesty [King Ferdinand VII] was disposed [willing] to make of the Floridas." As he said, "I will not advise His Majesty to make any settlement unless it fixes safe and permanent limits west of the Mississippi." Adams replied, "If that's the way it is, we can take the Rio Bravo del Norte for a frontier." "Better still the Mississippi," Onís replied, making clear that Spain was not about to give up any more western territory than necessary.

THE MELISH MAP

The map that John Quincy Adams and Don Luis de Onís used to formulate the agreement that became the Transcontinental Treaty was the most current map of the United States. Drawn by cartographer John Melish and published on January 1, 1818, the *Map of the United States and the Contiguous British and Spanish Possessions* was not like the maps of the United States in use today. Although Melish had drawn the map to scale, he worked more from his imagination than from careful surveys and detailed knowledge of the region. Few people had actually seen the territory represented on the map, and Melish himself knew very little about the geography of that vast western country. As a result, the map illustrated rivers flowing where in reality the land was dry. Similarly, the map indicated mountains in regions that are actually flat. Thus, using Melish's map to draw territorial boundaries was a great leap into the unknown.

⚊ A Critical Time ⚊

The days between July 11 and July 16, 1818, were critical in the negotiations between Adams and Onís. Without encouragement from Adams, Baron de Neuville intervened in the talks. He tried to persuade the Spanish to moderate their demands so as not to provoke the Americans into recognizing the independence of the rebellious Spanish colonies in South America. After the wars of Napoléon Bonaparte, which had ended in 1815, European rulers wanted to prevent war and revolution in Europe. Accordingly, they did not wish to encourage wars from starting (even elsewhere) in the fear that they might spread. Moreover, if de Neuville supported the Americans against Spain, he hoped that in exchange, the Americans would oppose British ambitions in the Caribbean, where France had interests of its own to protect. In a letter to Onís, de Neuville criticized the actions of Andrew Jackson, whom he ridiculed as a "*Napoléon des bois*" (a "Napoléon of the woods" or a backwoods Napoléon). However, he told Onís that despite what Jackson had done, the French could not support Spanish claims. Spain must yield to the Americans, said de Neuville. The French minister's advice only succeeded in making Onís angrier.

That same summer, the American minister to Spain, George W. Erving, reported from Madrid that Jackson's invasion of Florida had thrown the Spanish government into a crisis. Intelligent and capable, if somewhat impatient and unpredictable, Erving was at a loss about what to do, for he did not understand Spanish royal politics. This would have been

Napoléon Bonaparte, who was crowned emperor in 1804, is seen here in this full-length portrait by famous French artist Jacques-Louis David. Painted in 1812, the image shows Bonaparte regally dressed in the most fashionable of French clothing for men. Ultimately, Napoléon was exiled to the island of Elba (pictured below). His tomb can be viewed at Les Invalides in Paris, France.

difficult for anyone in Erving's position since the Spanish king, Ferdinand VII, and the foreign minister, José Garcia de Leon y Pizarro, constantly worked against one another. While Pizarro was trying to cede Florida to the United States on the best possible terms, Ferdinand was doing everything in his power to make certain that Pizarro could not offer Florida to the Americans. On December 17, 1817, Ferdinand had granted almost the whole of East Florida to two of his court favorites, the Duke de Alagón and the Count de Puñonrostro. A little more than a month later, on January 25, 1818, Ferdinand made an additional grant of Florida land to another favorite, Don Pedro de Vargas. As a consequence of the king's actions, most of Florida no longer belonged to the Spanish monarchy. Instead, it was in private hands. When Erving learned what Ferdinand had done, he wrote immediately to inform Adams. Much to his dismay, Adams did not pay close attention to Erving's dispatch or else did not understand its significance.

⌐ Onís's Delays ⌐

Throughout the summer, Onís resisted the pressure that Adams and de Neuville exerted. He did not meet with Adams again until October 24, 1818. And then, he only repeated his previous demands, which he already knew the Americans would never accept. President Monroe finally lost his patience. He instructed Adams to settle matters with Spain or else end negotiations. Adams put forth a new and final proposal. In exchange for Florida, the Americans would agree to a boundary line drawn from the point at which the Sabine River emptied into the Gulf of Mexico and extended west to the Pacific along the 41st parallel. Onís accepted Adams's boundary as far north as the Red River. However, he thought that the line should then run north to the Missouri River. In his reply to Onís's counterproposal, delivered on October 31, Adams politely withdrew all offers of a settlement. However, contrary to Monroe's instructions, he left open the possibility of continuing negotiations.

⸗ A Changing Situation ⸗

Throughout January and the first half of February 1819, Adams and Onís resumed their debate about the boundary, and Baron de Neuville acted as an intermediary. However, the circumstances in which these discussions took place had changed since the last meeting in October. Although neither Adams nor Onís were aware of it in the fall, on September 14, 1818, Ferdinand VII had removed the able foreign minister Pizarro from office and sent Pizarro and his family away to a distant home in Spain. Onís wondered whether the instructions that Pizarro had sent him were still valid. Had the policies of his government toward Florida and the western territories changed as a result of Pizarro's removal?

By February, Onís realized that the Spanish could not count on any help from the British in settling the boundary dispute. Nor could Spain keep the United States from recognizing the independence of the Spanish colonies in South America. In a letter to Erving written in November, Adams had heaped contempt upon Spain and had also challenged Great Britain—a challenge that the British leaders, for reasons of their own, had chosen to overlook. The British foreign secretary, Robert Stewart, Viscount Castlereagh, did not wish to go to war against the United States, even if it meant overlooking General Jackson's execution of two British subjects. Castlereagh welcomed the more peaceful economic and political relations with the Americans, which had begun after the War of 1812. He would not allow anything, not even Jackson's acts, to damage or disrupt the peace.

The Commercial Convention of 1815 had removed all restrictions on English-American trade, except British restrictions on American commerce with the West Indies. An agreement signed in 1817 by Richard Rush, the acting secretary of state, and Charles Bagot, the British minister to the United States, provided that the United States and Great Britain would limit the size of their naval forces on the Great Lakes. According to the terms of the Rush-Bagot Treaty, the Americans and the British were each permitted one ship on Lake Ontario and two ships on the other Great Lakes. The Rush-Bagot Treaty (see page 55 for a partial transcription) thus began the process that led to the permanent demilitarization, or ending of military protection, along the United States–Canadian border. This is still the longest unprotected border in the world.

In 1818, after he became secretary of state, Adams drew up the Convention (agreement) of 1818, which covered three major issues. First, it reopened the waters off the coast of Newfoundland and Labrador to American fishermen. Second, it fixed the 49th parallel as the northern boundary of the Louisiana Territory. Third, it established the joint British-American occupation of the Oregon Territory, the actual

This color lithograph by artist Louis Breton illustrates cod fishermen off the coast of Newfoundland in their sailing vessels. Cod fishing was a very important industry for what would later become New England and the Canadian maritime provinces of Nova Scotia and Newfoundland.

boundary of which was left unsettled. Neither the British nor the Americans realized that these peaceful negotiations would become a model for future English-American relations. Like many other British statesmen, Viscount Castlereagh had decided that it was useful both politically and economically for the British to deal with independent countries in South America. This way, each government would be free to establish its own relations with Great Britain. Once Onís grasped Castlereagh's thinking and understood British interests, he gave up any hope of British intervention against the United States and moved toward a settlement.

⇌ An Agreement at Last ⇌

Events also motivated Adams to quickly resolve outstanding differences with Spain. Adams and Monroe faced criticism

Henry Clay is featured here in a portrait by Matthew Harris Jouett dating from 1818. Although Jouett painted many images of Clay, he only asked his subject to pose for him once. Born in Virginia, Clay (1777–1852) later moved to Lexington, Kentucky, where he lived for the rest of his life.

from members of Congress. On February 8, 1819, Henry Clay, the Speaker of the House of Representatives, and William H. Crawford, the secretary of the treasury, made a motion, or proposal, that they hoped would discredit the Monroe administration. They criticized Monroe and Adams for Jackson's conduct in Florida and for allowing the negotiations with Spain to stall. However, they failed in convincing Congress.

Within a week, Adams and Onís resumed direct talks and quickly eliminated most of the points of their disagreement. Pressured by Monroe to draw up an agreement, Adams reluctantly gave in to Onís's demand to set the east-west boundary dividing Spanish and American territory at the 42nd parallel. On February 20, the negotiations came to an end. This occurred when Onís withdrew his insistence that the north-south boundary fall in the middle of the Sabine, Red, Platte, and Arkansas rivers, as was the diplomatic convention, and accepted the riverbanks as the boundary line. On February 22, 1819, Adams and Onís added their signatures to the Transcontinental Treaty. Two days later, on

February 24, the Senate approved the treaty. In his diary, Adams triumphantly noted, "The acquisition of Florida has long been an object of earnest desire for this country. The acknowledgement of a definite line of boundary to the South Sea forms a great epoch in our history."

s of Spain or of her Colonies, sha
rs to the ports of Pensacola and
out paying other or higher duties

4

The Transcontinental Treaty

ith the stroke of a pen, the United States acquired Florida and settled the western boundary. Adams's intelligent diplomatic negotiations with Onís had paid off for the United States. Having received approval from the Senate, the treaty only had to receive the permission of the Spanish cortes (the Spanish congress and the Spanish crown). At last the question of Florida and the western boundary could be put to rest.

⚌ Terms of the Treaty ⚌

The Transcontinental Treaty consisted of sixteen articles. Article I proclaimed peace and friendly relations between the United States government and the Spanish monarchy. Article II was one of the most important. In it, the king of Spain formally surrendered "all the territories *which belong to him*, situated east of the Mississippi, known by the name of East and West Florida." Under this article, the United States held the legal right to Florida.

Article III defined the western boundary between the United States' and Spain's territory. The boundary began at

Art. 2.

S. M. C. cede á los Estados Unidos, en toda propiedad y Soberania, todos los territorios que le pertenecen situados al Este del Mi-
sisipi, conocidos bajo el nombre de Florida Occidental y Florida Ori-
ental. Son comprehendidos en este articulo las yslas adyacentes depen-
dientes de dichas dos Provincias, los Sitios, Plazas publicas, terrenos
valdios, edificios publicos, fortificaciones, casernas y otros edificios que
no sean propiedad de algun individuo particular, los Archivos y documentos directamente relativos á la propiedad y soberania de las
mismas dos Provincias. Dichos Archivos y documentos se entregarán
á los Comisarios ú Oficiales de los Estados Unidos debidamente auto-
rizados para recibirlos.

Pictured above is the Spanish copy of Article II of the Transcontinental Treaty. This document was written on cotton rag paper. For an English transcription, see page 54.

the mouth of the Sabine River and continued north along the western bank, westward along the banks of the Red River, and then north to the Arkansas River. The article also granted navigation rights of the Sabine, Red, and Arkansas rivers to Spanish settlers.

Article IV created a commission with representatives from Spain and the United States to survey the boundary. It was almost thirty years before the boundary was formally marked. By that time, it hardly mattered, because by the late 1840s, the United States controlled Texas, New Mexico, Arizona, and California.

Religious freedom for residents of Florida was granted under Article V. So was the right of any person to move

THE IMPORTANT COMMA

The meaning of Article II rested on the punctuation of a single sentence. The article stated, "His Catholic Majesty cedes [gives up] to the United States, in full property and sovereignty, all the territories which belong to him, situated to the eastward of the Mississippi, known by the name of East and West Florida." Onís wanted the article to reflect the ceding of the territories then known as East and West Florida. This meant placing a comma between the words "territories" and "which." If Adams accepted this punctuation, he would have been admitting that the United States had taken West Florida without title. Adams refused to accept Onís's suggestion. As a result, there is no comma between the two words in the final document.

from Florida to Spanish territory. Article VI promised that the Florida territory would be incorporated into the United States as soon as possible.

Articles VII and VIII formally spelled out the plan for Spanish evacuation of its military personnel from Florida and declared "null and void" (or worthless) any royal land grants made before January 24, 1818. This meant that the United States did not recognize the validity of any land that the Spanish king had given away. Under Articles IX, X, and XI, the United States and Spain renounced all previous debts and other financial claims against each other. The United States also promised to pay for damages that Spanish soldiers and civilians in Florida had suffered as the result of Jackson's

This hand-colored aquatint (a printmaking technique) depicts members of the Spanish infantry equipped with their artillery. This print was published circa 1800 in Vienna. Though the British soldiers had little to say about the Spanish soldiers that was positive, they later changed their minds and recruited many for their own army.

invasion. Finally, the United States government agreed to pay the claims of American citizens against Spain.

Pinckney's Treaty of 1795 was the focus of Article XII. Among other things, this treaty had guaranteed the Americans right of deposit along the Mississippi River. This meant that American ships could unload cargo freely along river ports without paying a tax to Spain. Under the new treaty, the 1795 treaty was declared null and void, as the United States owned that territory. Adams also included a clause stating that if either Spain or the United States went to war against a third country, the neutral country's right to trade with the enemy was acknowledged. This clause became known as the "Adams clause" and would become a standard part of future American maritime, or sea, treaties.

Articles XIII, XIV, and XV dealt more specifically with naval matters. These articles included provisions for the return of all deserters from the ships of the United States or Spain to their respective countries. The United States was to make a formal declaration that it had never received compensation from the French for "spoilations on American ships in Spanish territorial waters." This meant that the Spanish could collect money from the French for damages to Spanish ships. Article XV provided Spain with the right to bring ships and goods to the ports of Pensacola and St. Augustine, Florida, without paying higher duties than American ships or goods of the same kind. Finally, Article XVI gave both countries six months in which to approve the treaty.

⌐ Unexpected Trouble ⌐

John Quincy Adams always believed that the worst was going to happen. After the Transcontinental Treaty had been signed and ratified, Adams wrote in his diary that he had "a vague, general, and superstitious impression that this treaty was too great a blessing not to be followed shortly by something to allay it." In this case, Adams's characteristic pessimism was well-founded, and he did not have long to wait for bad news to arrive.

On March 8, 1819, Speaker Clay, who was among Adams's most loyal political allies, informed President Monroe that he had learned from reliable sources that at the time Congress ratified the Transcontinental Treaty, Florida was no longer a possession of Spain. Most of it was in private hands, Clay explained. It had been ceded in royal grants from Ferdinand VII to the Duke de Alagón, the Count de Puñonrostro, and Señor Don Pedro de Vargas.

According to Article VII of the treaty, all land grants in Florida made before January 24, 1818, were valid and had to be honored by the United States. Adams urgently reviewed the correspondence of George Erving, the American minister to Spain, in order to discover evidence of the grants. To his sorrow, he found it. Perhaps Adams had not understood the significance of Erving's letter when he first read it. More likely, Adams had read it quickly and mistook the date. This caused confusion as to when exactly the captain-general of Cuba was authorized to transfer possession of the Count de Puñonrostro's Florida lands to his agents, which was on February 6, 1818. Adams believed the date for the transfer to be December 17, 1817. Vargas had received his grant after January 24, 1818, but Puñonrostro's and Alagón's grants were legitimate. Under the terms of the treaty, the Spanish had many grounds on which to contest the transfer of Florida to the United States.

Adams was devastated, though Monroe tried to reassure him. Monroe promised that if Ferdinand refused to annul or end the grants, he would have no trouble persuading Congress to authorize taking Florida by force. Monroe also

Famous Spanish painter and printmaker Francisco de Goya created this portrait of King Ferdinand VII around 1814. Goya, who was appointed court painter in 1799, was influenced by the paintings of masters such as Rembrandt and his fellow Spaniard, Diego Rodríguez de Silva Velázquez.

offered the possibility of the Texas territory as a reward to compensate for American costs and losses. Matters soon went from bad to worse. John Forsyth of Georgia, the new American minister to Spain, could secure neither the assurance that the Spanish government would void the king's Florida land grants nor the guarantee that it would ratify the treaty itself. As Forsyth wrote to Adams in September, Spanish authorities "insist on the validity of the grants and want some explanation relative to their colonial possessions." In other words, the Spanish sought a guarantee that the United States would not recognize the independence of the revolutionary governments in South America. Forsyth believed that he could accomplish nothing more. Because of this, he asked to be relieved of his ministerial duties.

⚊ A Breakthrough ⚊

However, events in which the Americans played no role brought an unexpected reversal in their fortunes and secured Spanish acceptance of the Transcontinental Treaty. King Ferdinand had gathered an army in Cádiz in preparation for an invasion of South America. In 1820, a rebellion broke out among Spanish officers and quickly spread to Madrid. This forced Ferdinand to issue a new constitution. When the Spanish uprising inspired rebellions in Portugal and the Kingdom of the Two Sicilies (Southern Italy), other European powers came to regard the Spanish government as unstable. They viewed Spain as a dangerous source of revolution. Spanish authorities realized that under these circumstances, Spain could expect no help in the dispute with the United

States. Given their serious domestic problems and their growing diplomatic isolation, the Spanish could not afford to carry on a feud with the Americans. The Spanish could delay no longer. On October 5, 1820, the Spanish cortes nullified, or overturned, Ferdinand's Florida land grants; on October 24, Ferdinand VII signed the Transcontinental Treaty. With only four negative votes, the United States Senate again ratified the treaty on February 19, 1821. On February 22, Secretary of State Adams exchanged formal documents of ratification with Don Francisco Vives, the new Spanish minister to the United States.

⌒ The Significance of the Transcontinental Treaty ⌒

In taking advantage of Spain's troubles over its rebellious South American colonies, Adams put himself in a stronger bargaining position and came away from the negotiations with most of what he wanted. By giving up Texas, which Onís had desperately wanted to preserve for Spain, the United States received Florida and gained a stronger foothold in the west. The treaty thus added to the territory under American control and improved national security of the United States.

For John Quincy Adams, the Transcontinental Treaty was a diplomatic triumph and remains among the most brilliant and successful accomplishments in American history. For Adams, though, the treaty represented much more than a personal victory. With it, he had gone a long way toward achieving his ambition of establishing a continental empire for the United States. And this was what he thought was the key to America's future. Adams's skillful settlement of the western boundary opened a new chapter in the history of the United States. Adams envisioned that westward expansion would one day extend American dominion from the Atlantic to the Pacific and make the United States a truly great nation.

Timeline

≋ **1803** Louisiana Purchase completed between the United States and France.

≋ **1810** Secretary of State James Madison orders that American jurisdiction extend to the Perdido River in Florida.

≋ **1812** Congress formally annexes West Florida between the Pearl and Perdido rivers on May 14.

≋ **1815** Onís officially received by the United States government in December.

≋ **1816** James Monroe becomes fifth president of the United States; John Quincy Adams is appointed secretary of state.

≋ **1817** James Monroe tours the country, proclaiming the "era of good feelings."

≋ **1817** Secretary of War John C. Calhoun orders Andrew Jackson, commander of the American army in the southwest, to cross into Florida and stop the Seminole threat.

≋ **1818** Jackson crosses into Spanish Florida, taking control of a Spanish fort, St. Marks, and the capital of Spanish Florida, Pensacola.

≋ **1818** Monroe learns the news of Jackson's invasion on June 18. Cabinet sessions are held for a week, and all are opposed to Jackson's actions except John Quincy Adams and Monroe.

≋ **1819** While Onís delays, Monroe threatens war with Spain. Onís is instructed by Spain to concede Florida and finish the negotiations to avoid war.

≋ **1819** Adams-Onís Treaty is signed on February 22. The treaty establishes new boundaries from the Sabine to the Red, Arkansas, and Platte rivers, then by the 42nd parallel to the Pacific.

≋ **1821** Treaty ratification is delayed until 1821 due to last-minute Spanish land grants in East Florida.

Primary Source Transcriptions

Page 7 and 43: Excerpt from the Transcontinental Treaty

Transcription

The United States of America and His Catholic Majesty, desiring to consolidate, on a permanent basis, the friendship and good correspondence which happily prevails between the two parties, have determined to settle and terminate all their differences and pretensions, by a treaty, which shall designate, with precision, the limits of their respective bordering territories in North America . . .

ARTICLE I

There shall be a firm and inviolable peace and sincere friendship between the United States and their citizens and His Catholic Majesty, his successors and subjects, without exception of persons or places.

ARTICLE II

His Catholic Majesty cedes to the United States, in full property and sovereignty, all the territories which belong to him, situated to the eastward of the Mississippi, known by the name of East and West Florida. The adjacent islands dependent on said provinces, all public lots and squares, vacant lands, public edifices, fortifications, barracks, and other buildings, which are not private property, archives and documents, which relate directly to the property and sovereignty of said provinces, are included in this article. The said archives and documents shall be left in possession of the commissaries or officers of the United States, duly authorized to receive them.

ARTICLE III

The boundary-line between the two countries, west of the Mississippi, shall begin on the Gulph of Mexico, at the mouth of the river Sabine, in the sea, continuing north, along the western bank of that river, to the 32d degree of latitude; thence, by a line due north, to the degree of latitude where it strikes the Rio Roxo of Nachitoches, or Red River; then following the course of the Rio Roxo westward, to the degree of longitude 100 west from London and 23 from Washington; then, crossing the said Red River, and running thence, by a line due north, to the river Arkansas; thence, following the course of the southern bank of the Arkansas, to its source, in latitude 42 north; and thence, by that parallel of latitude, to the South Sea. The whole being as laid down in Melish's map of the United States, published at Philadelphia, improved to the first of January, 1818. But if the source of the Arkansas River shall be found to fall north or south of latitude 42, then the line shall run from the said source due south or north, as the case may be, till it meets the said parallel of latitude 42, and thence, along the said parallel, to the South Sea: All the islands in the Sabine, and the said Red and Arkansas Rivers, throughout the course thus described to belong to the United States; but the use of the waters, and the navigation of the Sabine to the sea, and of the said rivers Roxo and Arkansas, throughout the extent of the said boundary, on their respective banks, shall be common to the respective inhabitants of both nations.

The two high contracting parties agree to cede and renounce all their rights, claims, and pretensions to the territories described by the said line, that is to say: The United States hereby cede to His Catholic Majesty, and renounce forever, all their rights, claims, and pretensions, to the territories lying west and south of the above-described line; and, in like manner, His Catholic Majesty cedes to the said United States all his rights, claims, and pretensions to any territories east and north of the said line, and for himself, his heirs, and successors, renounces all claim to the said territories forever.

Page 25: Excerpt from page 1 of Memoir Upon the Negotiations Between Spain and the United States of America, Which Led to the Treaty of 1819

Transcription
. . . The disagreements which gave rise to the negotiation with the United States of America, may be said to have taken their origin from the treaty of amity, limits, and navigation, concluded in 1795. This treaty signed by Don Manuel Godoy without any geographical knowledge of the countries upon which it turned, nor the mutual interests of the powers, gave to the American territory about one degree, in the whole extent of the dividing line between the Floridas and the territory of that Republick, from East to West, and put into their hands the most fertile lands that belonged to the Floridas, the most beautiful rivers that flowed from Georgia and Mississippi, the important post of Natches, and other fortifications that served for our defence of the Floridas against the United States . . .

Page 38: Excerpt from the Rush-Bagot Treaty, 1818

Transcription
The naval force to be maintained upon the American lakes, by His Majesty and the government of the United States, shall henceforth be confined to the following vessels on each side; that is—

On lake Ontario, to one vessel not exceeding one hundred tons burden, and armed with tie eighteen pound cannon.

On the upper lakes, to two vessels, not exceeding like burden each, and armed with like force.

On the waters of lake Champlain, to one vessel not exceeding like burden, and armed with like force.

All other armed vessels on these lakes shall be forthwith dismantled, and no other vessels of war shall be there built or armed.

If either party should hereafter be desirous of annulling this stipulation, and should give notice to that effect to the other party it shall cease to be binding after the expiration of six months from the date of such notice.

The naval force so to be limited shall be restricted to such services as will, in no respect, interfere with the proper duties of the armed vessels of the other party.

s of Spain or of her Colonies, sha
rs to the ports of Pensacola and
out paying other or higher duties

Glossary

annul To cancel or terminate.

armada A fleet of warships.

buccaneer A pirate; someone who robs at sea.

claim A right to something, especially land.

condemned Pronounced guilty.

conquistadores Conquerors; in Spanish history, leaders in the Spanish conquest of America.

contiguous Adjoining.

counterproposal A returned offer after the first offer is rejected.

deserter One who abandons military duty without permission.

discredit To dishonor or shame.

duties Taxes levied on goods imported into a country.

fraud An act of deceiving or misrepresenting.

fugitive slaves Slaves who had run away to escape slavery.

Holy Roman Emperor The ruler of an empire that included German and Italian territories and existed from the ninth or tenth century to 1806.

manifest destiny A mid-nineteenth-century belief that expansion to the Pacific was America's destiny.

maritime Having to do with nautical or naval matters.

Pinckney Treaty A treaty made between the United States and Spain in 1795. It recognized the 31st parallel as the boundary to the south of the American territory, the free navigation of the Mississippi River by U.S. citizens, and the privilege of deposit. The treaty affirmed the principle of neutral rights (meaning that in times of war, neutral or non-committed nations can trade with any country involved in the conflict), and each side agreed to restrain the Indians within their borders from attacking the territory of the other.

precedent Something done or said that serves as an example or rule to justify a similar act.

reign To possess royal authority over a country.

will The power to control one's own actions.

worthy Having value.

For More Information

Florida Historical Society
435 Brevard Avenue
Cocoa, FL 32922
Web site: http://www.florida-historical-soc.org

U.S. Capitol Historical Society
200 Maryland Avenue NE
Washington, DC 20002
Web site: http://www.uschs.org/04_history/subs_articles/
04e_09.html

WEB SITES

Due to the changing nature of Internet links, the Rosen
Publishing Group, Inc., has developed an online list of Web
sites related to the subject of this book. This site is updated
regularly. Please use this link to access the list:

http://www.rosenlinks.com/psat/trtr

For Further Reading

Burgan, Michael. *John Quincy Adams*. New York, NY: Compass
    Point Books, 2003.
Heinrichs, Ann. *Florida*. New York, NY: Children's Press, 1998.
Knotts, Bob. *Florida History*. New York, NY: Heinemann
    Library, 2002.
Levy, Debbie. *John Quincy Adams*. Minneapolis, MN: Lerner
    Publishing Group, 2004.

...s of Spain or of her colonies, shall...
...rs to the ports of Pensacola and St...
...out paying other or higher duties on

Bibliography

Bemis, Samuel Flagg. *John Quincy Adams and the Foundations of American Foreign Policy*. New York, NY: Alfred A. Knopf, 1965.

Brooks, Philip C. *Diplomacy and the Borderland: The Adams-Onís Treaty of 1819*. Berkeley, CA: University of California Press, 1939.

Hecht, Marie. *John Quincy Adams: A Personal History of an Independent Man*. New York, NY: Macmillan, 1972.

Nagel, Paul C. *John Quincy Adams: A Public Life, A Private Life*. New York, NY: Alfred A. Knopf, 1997.

Nevins, Alan, ed. *The Diary of John Quincy Adams, 1794–1845*. New York, NY: Frederick Ungar Publishing Co., 1969.

Primary Source Image List

Index

ABOUT THE AUTHOR

Meg Greene is a writer and historian with degrees in history and historic preservation. She is the author of more than twenty-five books and numerous magazine articles. Two of her books have won awards: *Slave Young, Slave Long* was recognized as an 1999 Honor Book from the Society of School Librarians International for Grades 7–12, and *Buttons, Bones, and the Organ Grinder's Monkey* was chosen as a 2001 New York Public Library Best Book for Teens. Ms. Greene makes her home in Virginia.

PHOTO CREDITS

Cover, p. 16 Library of Congress, Prints and Photographs Division; pp. 6, 11, 20, 32 Library of Congress, Geography and Map Division; pp. 7, 43 National Archives and Records Administration; p. 10 Topkapi Palace Museum, Istanbul, Turkey/Bridgeman Art Library; p. 12 © Scala/Art Resource, NY; pp. 19, 24 © National Portrait Gallery, Smithsonian Institution/Art Resource, NY; p. 25 Milstein Division of United States History, Local History & Genealogy, The New York Public Library, Astor, Lenox and Tilden Foundations; p. 27 © Brooklyn Museum of Art, New York/Bridgeman Art Library; p. 35 (top) akg-images; p. 35 (bottom) Musee de la Ville de Paris, Musee Carnavalet, Paris, France/Giraudon/Bridgeman Art Library; p. 39 the Mariners' Museum, Newport News, VA; p. 40 courtesy of the Diplomatic Reception Rooms, U.S. Dept of State, Washington, DC; p. 45 Anne S. K. Brown Military Collection, Brown University Library; p. 48 Prado, Madrid, Spain/Bridgeman Art Library.

Designer: Evelyn Horovicz; Editor: Annie Sommers
Photo Researcher: Jeffrey Wendt